A Goal Diggin Goddess's Guide to Building Her Empire: 12 Laws to organize your Schedule and Create Your Tomorrow, TODAY. 2nd edition
© 2018 by Cräv Life Consulting, LLC All rights reserved.

www.cravlife.com

Published by Cráv Life Consulting, LLC

Editor: Latia Harris

cravlifeth@gmail.com

All rights reserved. No part of this publication, including forms and framework may be reproduced, stored in a retrieval system, or transmitted in any form, or by any means without the prior written permission and consent of the publisher.

Cover Art by: Octavia Harris

Contents

Reset and Learn	4
Law #1	6
Law #2	8
Law #3	9
Law #4	10
Law #5	11
Law #6	13
Law #7	13
Law #8	14
Law #9	14
Law #10	15
Law #11	15
Law #12	17
Extra	18
Your Schedule	20
References	27

Dear Beautiful Soul,

This book is dedicated to the female entrepreneurs of the world who have a gift to share with the world. This book was created because after 10 years as an entrepreneur, my schedule was a mess. I was always 15 minutes late to everything and anxiety was my way of life. I was great at what I did, but I had a hard time keeping things organized.

How many of you have purchased and downloaded planners and they simply don't work for you? I have downloaded and purchased so many organizers yet, I couldn't find one that worked with me. Nothing felt like it covered all the small details I needed to keep up with IN MY BUSINESS. More importantly, I was tired of my todo list. It was mixed with projects from work and home plus, I never felt motivated to complete the list.

The lack of a sec schedule caused years of procrastination. Now, if you have read Mel Robbins, the 5 second rule, you will know that there are two kinds of procrastination, and mine was the bad version. I needed a something to work with my needs. I spent time reading books on how to better your schedule, articles, and interview other entrepreneurs to get an idea of their needs as well. That is how these laws came about. I hope you enjoy it and it helps your business grow.

As you create your schedule and it starts to work for you, please tag us on social media and share your story with the hashtag #GoalDigginGoddess #CravLifeare two kinds of procrastination, and mine was the bad version. I needed a something to work with my needs. I spent time reading books on how to better your schedule, articles, and interview other entrepreneurs to get an idea of their needs as well. That is how these laws came about. I hope you enjoy it and it helps your business grow.

As you create your schedule and it starts to work for you, please tag us on social media and share your story with the hashtag #GoalDigginGoddess #CravLife

Please join us on social media

Type #Cravlife in any Application or

Like us on Facebook:
https://www.facebook.com/cravlife/
Follow us on Twitter:
https://twitter.com/CravLife
Follow us on Instagram:
https://www.instagram.com/cravlife/
Subscribe on YouTube:
http://www.youtube.com/c/OctaviaCravLife
Connect on LinkedIn:
https://www.linkedin.com/in/octaviaharriscravlife/
Please join our Facebook Business group:
https://www.facebook.com/groups/thegoddessden1/
Listen on our Podcast
(Goal Diggin Goddess By Octavia Harris on any platform)
https://anchor.fm/goaldiggingoddess

With Love,
Octavia Harris, CEO & International Content & Marketing Strategist

Reset & Relearn

I created this process because my to-do list kept me up at night and scared me in the daytime. My to-do list left me feeling like I was stranded on an island surrounded by work, while being stuck in quick sand. I turned into a procrastinator who multi-tasked and neither is good.

Today, I am an anticipator who sleeps well, finds time for cleaning, cooking, family; runs a successful business, volunteers, and gives back daily. I always say, *"You do not have to let words like "overwhelmed" or "burnt out" be your minds description of yourself."* ~ Octavia Harris

"Burnout occurs when your body and mind can no longer keep up with the tasks you demand of them. Don't try to force yourself to do the impossible. Delegate time for important tasks, but always be sure to leave time for relaxation and reflection." ~ Del Suggs, Truly Leading: Lessons in Leadership

There is never a reason to rewrite history or recreate the wheel when it is working. You are here today because the information you know about scheduling are mixed in with some worldly beliefs that need to be reset and re-learned to build a life and schedule you love. This book focuses on my personal systems that have allowed me to create several 6-figure businesses, but I did not create these ideas alone.

My three main contributors are Kevin Kruse and his book, 15 Secrets Successful People Know about Time Management, David Allen's, Getting Things Done and The 7 Habits of Highly Effective People by Stephen Covey.

These three books have helped transform my clients, partners, and myself into power house CEO's, and it will do the same for you.

This book will allow you to plan your goals, day, year, and life, as you watch your-self achieve your wildest, biggest, most bodacious goals.

A Goal Diggin Goddess's Guide to Building Her Empire

Reset Your Laws

Law #1

Your brain is for brainstorming and thinking!

Use it to Prioritize your Projects, NOT to

rememebr your to-do list.

David Allen who wrote, Getting Things Done, explains this law. Your brain is one of the most amazing assets you have. Nurture it with water, food, exercise, and rest! Reset your mindset to no longer use your brain as your personal storage device that needs to remember everything.

What it should be used for:	What it is NOT for:
Brainstorming	Storage device
Strategies	Organizing time
Math	Juggling tasks
Re-Experiencing Pleasant Events	To-do list
Thinking Positive	Remembering Everything you need to do
Meditation	Filing Cabinet
Solving Puzzles	Calendar
Reading	Having conversations that result in anger
Chatting & Listening	Overthinking Operation = This is when your thoughts stop you from moving forward.
Invalidate Negative Thoughts	NUTS or Negative Unconscious Thinking
Learning, Stretching and Growing	Thinking about past pain (Unless you are working on healing at that time)

Do you want to be more efficient with your time? We always hear people say, "There isn't enough time in the day." Nevertheless, there is, because everywhere we look, we see ideas that people have put action behind to create the things we love the most. From your favorite apps, digital books, video games, to basketball players who practice for hours on end, and directors, actors, and actresses on your favorite TV shows. These people have found the secret to success and have mastered time management.

I understand how it can be to finally get in from of a project and not feel focused or ready to start it. The problem is, if you do not have your projects under control, your mind will prompt you to start thinking about other projects at the worst possible moments. Especially, when you are smack in the middle of important tasks or even worse, you todo list starts looping in your head so much, it drives you nuts and leads you to NUTS (Negative Unconscious Thinking.)

WHY?

If you give your mind the task of keeping up with your to-do list, you are doomed because your brain has no "TIME CLOCK." It cannot tell time, it does not understand time because time was created by man. Our brains spend the majority of its time trying to solve our problems, thats it's function. Organizing your to-do list, calendar, and everything in between, all while you need to be 100% focused on what you are actually doing. It cannot do both. Well, it can, but not efficiently.

Using your brain as a storage device can turn against you and make you feel self-doubt, like a failure, insufficient or worse, simply make you feel like you are a forgetful failure at life. So, keep a screenshot of this list to remind yourself of what your brain does, and what things must be organized, and written down so you can be more efficient. This will lead you to better time management, new peace of mind, free time, naps, gratitude for your time, and unlock potential you never knew you had because you will be crushing every task you write down.

Once you release your brain from the task remembering your to-do list, you will become more efficient because you will have a place to write down new ideas and thoughts that matter. To help your brain get adjusted to your new way of thinking, when a past task arises, you can immediately put it to rest by saying, "that project is taking care of, it is on my calendar" and go on about your day. Your brain will stop trying to fix your schedule problems and it can finally relax. Then you will be free to use 100% of your mind during tasks you work on.

Law #2

Clear your Thoughts and Create an "External Head Space."

Write this down: Create Your Lists using a journal or notebook, CRM application Asana, Daylite 6, Microsoft One Note, Note Keeps by Google, Apple Notes, Apple Reminders, journal, calendar (digital and/or physical) or anywhere else where you can carry it on you at all times and have quick access to it.

Create a place outside of your mind that is respsoble for all of your tasks and projects. A new place you can use as a storage system such as:

A notebook, CRM application, Microsoft One Note, Note Keeps by Google, Apple Notes, Apple Reminders, book, journal, calendar (digital and/or physical), or anywhere else where you can carry it on you and have quick access to it at all times.

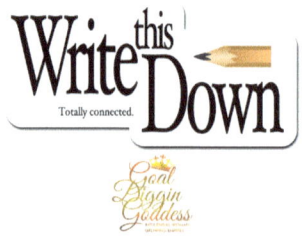

Law #3
Delete the Unnecessary… weekly, yes! Weekly!

In order to be efficient, entrepreneurs and thinkers must develop systems that help them stay efficient. Developing systems means creating a routine for how you do something all the time. This also means that if you start to slack off, you must grow your consistency muscle and keep tweaking your systems you create until they feel good to do and they work for you. Sometimes we think because something doesn't work or we don't keep at it that the item may be flawed. However, the real problem may be that we are not making changes slowly, giving things time and being consistent enough to see the change happen.

Deleting the Unnecessary means working on your schedule until it feels like "YOU" not a schedule. Meaning, if waking up 1 hour earlier isn't working, try just 30 minutes, then 45 minutes. Checking in on your systems and your schedule weekly Will allow you to keep it cleaned out, keep your todo list short every week and help you see that you have more time to do the things you've always wanted to spend time doing.

Each week, schedule a window of time to empty out your "External Head Space" or the place that you create this schedule. Delete what has been completed, moving what's next to your next steps list, adding any new ideas to your tabled list and moving some things from your tabled list to your next step list. You will start to see, you have more time for projects that have been on the back burner for so long, you've created a fear around them.

Decluttering will allow you:
* Peace of mind.
* To trust you are not forgetting anything.
* Trust your intuition.
* Rest better
* Wake up without regret from the day before.

Declutter

* Have a set time and day of the week to do this at least once every two weeks but the experts and myself recommend weekly.

* You do not have to complete each task when you go over your

list, just tidy it up, and move things to where they belong. This is a system and systems run better if you maintenance them like oil changes to your vehicle.

* Look at what must be done next, learn to prioritize and put your tasks in order of must important.

* Place important tasks at the top of your Next Step list. If it is not important, remove it.

* If it can be delegated to another person, delegate it by adding a task to delegate it to another person on your Next Step List.

* If you can finalize it in under five minutes, do it NOW.

* If it needs to be filed, file it. If you do not have a place to put it, create a file for it digitally or physically.

* Write down the major things you completed on your WINS LIST.

Law #4

There is a place for everything and everything has a place, if not create one.

* When you declutter be sure to put things in categories as well as things in their place. This includes downloads, files, pictures, thoughts, and anything in between. If it has a place, you do not have to search for it.

* Create systems, this means, create a way to do things receptively until it becomes habit.

* Make decisions by asking yourself, "What is the next step in this project?" and put that step on the correct list: Projects List, Next Step List, Waiting on List, Future Me List or Wins List.

* Add a date and time to complete item. Accept you may need more time for it.

* If it is an appointment, or a deadline, put it on your calendar. Never use your mind to remember important times or dates.

* Put subscriptions and cancellations on your calendar.

* If your item has more than two actionable steps needed to complete it, add it to your projects list, and create the first actionable step to put on your next step list.
* Place undone things on your next week's Next Steps List

Law #5

Create a projects list. Create all projects with the END in mind.

The 7 Habits of Highly Effective People by Stephen Covey teaches how to define a project. Stephen says to define a project by the ideal outcome you plan to achieve and this will help you be more productive.

* Think about your project with the END in mind. When this project is finalized: OUTCOME.

* Every project should have a next step and that next step should be on your next Step List.

* Review and update weekly.

* Include things like being a better listener, books on how to learn, or be a better spouse.

> *"An effective project list will make you feel more in control of your life, productive, relaxed and focused. This is exactly how you reset your schedule and unlock the riches of life."* ~ Octavia Harris

A Project is:

An individual or collaborative set of tasks that is carefully planned, designed, and executed to achieve a particular outcome during a fixed amount of time and within a certain cost or budget. It is usually unique and requires two or more actionable steps.

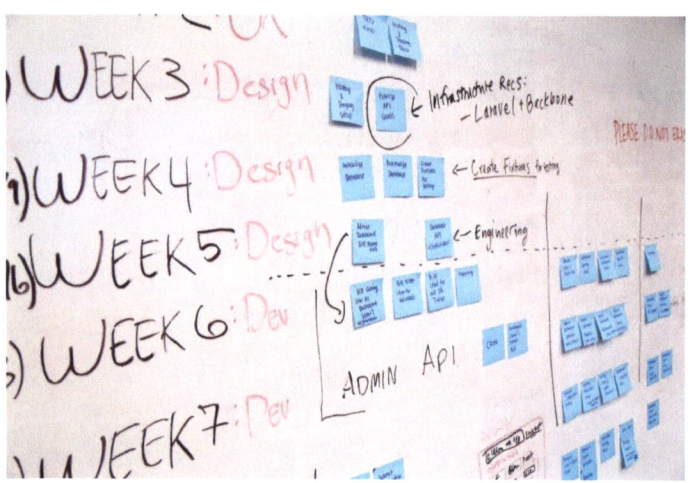

Law #6

Use a calendar. Period!

It can be digital, physical, or both; it must be done. Your brain is not a calendar and neither is your 100 sticky notes, jotted down notes, notes on your phone, nor notes on your hand or the back of napkins. The only way to know your schedule is to write it on a calendar.

Make sure to:

* Make your calendar the first thing you look at before your email, social media, or anything else. This should turn into a habit.

* Throw out every to-do list you have because they create an unrealistic expectation of your time and planning. This will always lead you to feeling of being unsuccessful in some way because your brain is trying to solve these problems on your list that are not prioritized or organized.

* Put any deadlines or due dates from your Projects List on your calendar.

* RESCHEDULE ANY UNDONE ITEMS TO A NEW DAY *

Law #7

Create a Next Step List

* The Next Step List is what must be done next in your open projects. This allows you to eliminate the feeling of being overwhelmed.

* This list should be at your fingertips or on your person at all times.

* When you have down time, you can always pull this list out and see what you can be done in the amount of time you have open.

* Have extra time? Ask yourself, "What can I do next? What can I do at this time? What can I do in this small window of time? What task can I accomplish in my current situation? What can I get done based on how much energy I have? Which task has priorities?"

* You can even get creative and categorize your Next Tasks lists:
    *Next Step List Phone Calls
    *Next Step List on Your Computer
    *Next Step List Under 15 Minutes

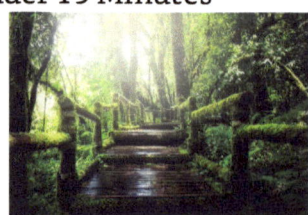

Law #8

Create a Waiting List

Life requires you have a team and work with people all the time. This means you are sometimes waiting on other people to finalize a task. The problem is, it is hard to remember how long it has been since you have heard from someone. Days can turn into weeks and by then, you are both avoiding each other.

This will allow you to:
* Notice when someone owes you pieces of a puzzle.
* Gently remind them that you are still waiting on their portion of the task.

Make sure to:
* Check this list weekly or even twice a week.
* Put any deadlines or needed reminders from your Waiting   List on your calendar.

Law #9

Create a Tabled Items List

Things you want more information about or waiting until you have more details to make a better decision.

Make sure to:

* Make reminders in your calendar to follow up on the details.

* To include new events, actives, books, movies, or even shows you would like to attend and wines to try.

* You can be relaxed or tedious with this. Just keep in mind you must keep it up.

Law #10

Create a Future Me List

This is a list of everything and I mean everything that you think you want to do. These things do not have a next action step. These are things you do not know how or even when it will be done, but you simply know you want to do it. This includes countries to visit, stages to grace, vacations to venture, your favorite teams tickets or 3-day yoga retreats.

Make sure to:

* Dream BIG! Think Big!
* Have big, hairy, and admirable plans and goals

Law #11

Structure: Structure your work area and your weekly review of your calendar, systems, and lists.

Make sure to:

* Develop a setup where you can access everything you need no matter where you are. Develop a system for when you work from workplace, home, or functional mobile system. This includes making sure you have good internet service if you are working outside of the workplace.

* What items do you need? What things do you not want to forget? Have a system of files you may always need to carry with you.

* Have a set date and time to review your calendars, systems and lists.

* Set a limit on how long it takes to update your lists. In the beginning, it may take you an hour, but your goal is to get it down to 30 minutes every Friday around 4pm. Be specific and make it the last thing you do for the week so you can spend your weekend stress free, knowing you are ready for Monday.

* Be religious about this update, this will bring trust and peace in your life. You will also feel and be more productive, have more control over your life, create comfort about what needs to be done, give your brain a break, and have a birds eye view of your life at all times.

Law #12

Throwing everything in your SACK!

Your SACK is the gifts your higher power or God gave you to be successful and be the best version yourself.

S = Self-love
A = Authenticity
C = Consistency
K = Knowledge

Be gentle and kind to yourself when you are not perfect at this. If you fall off, simply start over the same day or the next. Not Monday, the next day.

I know all things will work out which also includes knowing when to move and when to stand still.

Extra Tip

Learn the 7 Habits of Effective People by Dr. Stephen Covey

Habits:

1. <u>Sharpen your Saw:</u> Work smarter, not harder. Strive to be able to sustain all your tasks, have time for rest, family and continued efficiency.
2. <u>Be Proactive</u>: Reacting to life means, riding one bad wave to the next. Instead take charge, take responsibility for any part of what happens to you when life happens. No blaming.
3. <u>Begin with the End in Mind:</u> Begin each task, day, and even thinking with the end in mind, do not work aimlessly align your actions with an end goal. This means, saying no to things that serve you no purpose. Stop running to other peoples emergencies if they are not your own.
4. <u>Put First things First:</u> Do not allow urgent but unimportant or irrelevant to any of your goals or tasks to stop you from completing your tasks. If the heat goes out, call a heating and air condition man, work in the car, and connect to your own WIFI, if you have to. On New Year's Day, that is exactly what I did. Stay focused on what things you can do to make your ideal future your reality. Do not allow distractions to distract you.
5. <u>Think, WIN/WIN:</u> Do not try to get the most out of a deal. Try to make things equal by finding a happy medium for everyone. This will build strong relationships.
6. <u>Seek First to Understand, Then to be Understood:</u> Do not give your opinion or a recommendation unless it is asked

for and once you have listened ENTIRELY to what someone has said.

7. Synergize: All group efforts will always exceed any individual efforts. Build relationships and collaborations whenever possible.

Now, let's Build Your Schedule

Create Your Lists using a journal or notebook, CRM application Asana, Daylite 6, Microsoft One Note, Note Keeps by Google, Apple Notes, Apple Reminders, book, journal, calendar (digital and or physical) or anywhere else where you can carry it on you at all times and have quick access to it.

 * **Projects List -** This list is for all your tasks that have more than two actionable steps to complete.
* **Next Step List -** This is the next step of each of your project you are working on. Put the hardest and most important tasks first on your list. This means completing these things first in your day.
* **Waiting on List -** This list is for any projects you are awaiting on a response from others.
* **Tabled Items List -** Things you want more information about or waiting until you have more details to make a better decision.
* **Future Me List -** This is a list of things you plan to do one day. The things that do not have a date for or any actionable steps at this time. This is an important list because it can have things like "Present on stage with my mentor Les Brown." Big or small, write it down.
* **Wins List** -This list is a list of all things you are successful at from spending time with family, finalizing projects, writing five pages of your book, saying "No" to events, taking a day to rest, working 67 hours to finalize something big, getting up early 5 days in a row, or eating to nourish your body not to suppress emotional feelings. This list can be used at any time to remind you how Fucking Awesome you are.

TIPS:

* Work on one project at a time. Dedicate every bit of your momentum to completing that project before starting another.

* Always decide on a time to stop working.

* Assign a time daily to check and respond to emails.

* If you do work on multiple projects in one day, set a time period to work on each project. Example: Set you schedule to work for 40 mins, take a 15 min break and 5 mins to settle back and get back to work.

* Take a lunch break everyday.

* Sleep, eat and exercise for health.

My Annual Goals

email Octavia@cravlife.com to get a printbale copy

		What goals do I want to accomplish this year? What goals will make 2018 the best I have ever had?
		* Put an * beside the goals you want to work on this quarter
	1	
	2	
	3	
	4	
	5	
	6	
	7	
	8	
	9	
	10	
	11	
	12	
	13	
	14	
	15	
	16	

My Annual Goals

		What goals do I want to accomplish this year? What goals will make 2018 the best I have ever had?
		*Put an * beside the goals you want to work on this quarter
	1	
	2	
	3	
	4	
	5	
	6	
	7	
	8	
	9	
	10	
	11	
	12	
	13	
	14	
	15	
	16	

Daily Home Rituals

	Morning Time:	Total	
	Activity		**Allotted Time**
1			
2			
3			

4		
5		
6		
7		
8		

Evening Time:		**Total**
	Activity	Allotted Time
1		
2		
3		
4		
5		
6		
7		

Daily Workday Rituals

	Activity	Allotted Time
	Start Workday	
	End Workday	

Day:　　　　　Date:　　/　　/

☑		**Daily Top 3** (What are my top 3 tasks to complete today?)
	1	
	2	
	3	

☑	Next Steps Must DO
☑	Other Tasks

Octavia Harris Harris

Weekly Review

	My Big Wins (Top accomplishments for the week)
1	
2	
3	
4	
5	

Lessons Learned
What can I do better or differently? How will I adjust MY behavior?

Weekend/ Days off Optimization

Rest

How much sleep would I like to get?	Desired Hours	Day 1	Day 2
Would I like to take a nap? ☒ Yes ☒ No	If so, how long?		

What strategies will I put in place to make sure I get the right amount of sleep?

Relationships

List 3 to 5 relationships that you want to improve. What does quality time look like with them?

	Who	Activity	When

Works Cited

Allen, D. (2015). *Getting Things Done: The Art of Stress-Free Productivity Kindle Edition*. Penguin Books; Revised edition.

Covey, S. R. (2004). *The 7 Habits of Highly Effective People: Powerful Lessons in Personal Change*. Free Press; Revised edition.

Kruse, K. (2015). *15 Secrets Successful People Know About Time Management: The Productivity Habits of 7 Billionaires, 13 Olympic Athletes, 29 Straight-A Students, and 239 Entrepreneurs*. The Kruse Group.

www.ingramcontent.com/pod-product-compliance
Lightning Source LLC
Chambersburg PA
CBHW040248220526
45473CB00001B/417